THE POWER OF TRANSFORMATION

INTERNAL RESTRUCTURING FOR RENEWED EMPOWERMENT

DR. LARRY D CARNES

LARRY CARNES MINISTRIES

The Power of Transformation

Larry D. Carnes – Larry Carnes Ministries, Inc.

Stone Mountain, GA

www.larrycarnesministries.org

drcarnes@larrycarnesministries.org

Unless otherwise identified, Scripture quotations are taken from the **King James Version**.

Scripture quotations marked **AMP** are taken from the **Amplified Version**.

Scripture quotations marked **AMPC** are taken from the **Amplified Classic Edition**.

Scripture quotations marked **MSG** are taken from the **Message Translation**.

Scripture quotations marked **Voice** are taken from the **Voice Translation**.

Scripture quotations marked **Darby** are taken from the **Darby Translation**.

Scripture quotations marked **ERV** are taken from the **Easy to Read Version**.

Scripture quotations marked **GWT** are taken from the **God's Word Translation**.

Scripture quotations marked **NLT** are taken from the **New Living Translation**.

Scripture quotations marked **HCSB** are taken from the **Holman Christian Standard Bible.**

Scripture quotations marked **CJB** are taken from the **Complete Jewish Bible.**

Cover Design & Interior Layout: EvyDani Books, LLC

ISBN: 978-0-578-93980-3 (paperback)

Printed in the United States of America

DEDICATION

This project is dedicated to the person of the Holy Spirit for who He is and to my bishop and pastor Archbishop Kirby Clements. Archbishop Clements' book Empty Temple, The Neglected Holy Spirit, ignited a fire within me that caused me to hunger and thirst for a more personal and intimate relationship with the Person of the Holy Spirit. That desire and passion was the catalyst for the powerful move of God that was experienced during a visit to Brazil, as God said, "I'm going to show you what Pentecost was like." We experienced the outpouring of the Holy Spirit as He filled, empowered, and transformed lives in every city and state that we visited.

CONTENTS

FOREWORD

Limited Psychology drives the limits of an individual's life because of its ability to signal victim or victory.

In light of this, one of the hardest things for a good leader to find is another great leader that can successfully pour into and pull out of them the virtues necessary to enhance their personal value.

Throughout this introspective appeal to the mind you will be constantly challenged to re-evaluate your thinking (the thoughts that determine your perceptibility). Also prepare yourself to explore the reigns of your beliefs as you discover that Dr. Larry Carnes is a masterful teacher on the power and principles of Transformation.

His unique teaching style captivates, motivates, and challenges students to press beyond mediocrity and excel in multiple areas of their lives for the Kingdom of God while thoroughly restructuring themselves for renewed empowerment. *The Power of Transformation* is an essential read for today's Kingdom leaders and citizenship.

Dr. Bishop Finace Bush Jr.

INTRODUCTION

A prophetic word to me on January 13, 1994. "I will peel you like a man peels a banana. For I will peel you here, and I am peeling you there, that the real treasure of the man might be revealed, and, yes, the peeling will be painful and has discomfort, but the fruit is so sweet." This is what God told me years ago. Little did I know that my process of transformation started without me knowing anything about transformation or the processes involved. How do you respond when God tells you to keep silent concerning events that have taken place that paint a negative picture of you? How do you respond when God tells you, "Do not open your mouth to defend yourself?" What do you do when God says, "I'll vindicate you? Will you trust and obey Him? I Am the Book. Your process of transformation will be painful; the rewards, however, will be greater than the pain if you stay the course.

The word transformation in Greek is translated as "metamorphosis," which means being changed into a totally different form.

Transformation is the key to a revitalized you. The revitalization is an internal transformation that is based on the implementation of the revelation received during your processes of transformation.

Behavior modification is normal. But, transformation challenges your normal and stretches you to become extraordinary. This book is life-altering and will challenge you to step outside of your comfort zone as you gain knowledge and an understanding of the severity of the need to be transformed and live a transformed life.

As you survey the contents of this book and navigate its chapters, you will undoubtedly face several defining moments that will challenge you to make critical decisions and choices that will impact you; and set the course for the remainder of your life. Every situation that we face in life is a defining moment that's designed to elevate our consciousness, and bring us to a higher dimension of awareness as we uncover and discover our value and purpose.

You are full of greatness. The world is waiting for you to come forth as the manifested word that is written about within the pages of your life's purpose. It's time to give birth to your dreams and make them become your reality. Are you willing to endure the discomfort and pain of transformation, which fosters transformation within you and the world?

The Kingdom of God is within you. As you uncover and discover your true self within the context of who God created you to be, and are awakened to your assignment to be the extension of God's governmental authority on the Earth, you give place to the I Am that's within you. Your eschatology, (the reason for your existence, your life assignment) is to recolonize humanity and the Earth back to God.

1

THE POWER OF TRANSFORMATION

Welcome to *The Power of Transformation: Internal Restructuring for Renewed Empowerment,* where you will cease to be who you have been socialized and modified to be due to the environment that you have been exposed to; and will be transformed into who you were created to be in the Womb (Spirit) of God.

In his book; *God's Counterculture: The Strategy of the Kingdom of God that Transforms Your World,* Pastor Dan Rhodes wrights that God has a counterculture for every worldly culture that exists. Pastor Rhodes goes on to talk about "the Strategy of God's Counterculture to Discover Your Real Culture." He states that *"instead of falling into the trap that fosters the fallen nature, you should rise above it with your Redeemed Nature."* The biblical account given is that of Jesus's genealogy. As recorded in chapter one of Matthew, you'll discover that, despite the character flaws of your assessors, God can raise you as a testimony of His grace, mercy, and kind intentions. Your Real Culture can be lifted above your natural heritage. You must, however, be willing to surrender to the divine purpose and will of God for your life.

*The power of transformation is the internal restructuring of your
spiritual DNA!*

Matthew 17:1 *Six days later, three of them saw that glory. Jesus took
Peter and the brothers, James and John, and led them up a high
mountain. 2 His appearance changed from the inside out, right
before their eyes. Sunlight poured from his face. His clothes were
filled with light. (MSG)*

Matthew 17:1 *After six days Jesus took Peter, James, and his brother
John and led them up on a high mountain by themselves. 2 He
was transformed[a] in front of them, and His face shone like the
sun. Even His clothes became as white as the light. (HCSB)*

Is the transformation craze another fad that's going around the
religious community? Is it another temporary movement that's
destined to fizzle out after the initial excitement and fanfare wear off?
What is transformation? Is there a need to be transformed? How does
transformation take place, and how many are willing to submit to the
painful process of internal spiritual transformation? What are the
indicators, and who, other than God, reserves the right to decide if the
transformation has indeed taken place? How do you know when
you've stepped into your cocoon of isolation; and the
transformational process has started, and how do you know when the
process is complete? Let me end by asking this final question: How do
you prepare for this life-altering experience?

As I gave thought to my transformational journey and attempted to
answer these questions for myself, I thought about the caterpillar, the
frog, and the eagle, and how each has a transformational experience
that's different from the others. Making transformational
comparisons can be risky because your transformational experience
will be based on your assignment, life purpose, and personality, not

someone else's. The danger of making comparisons is that you may convince yourself that you aren't capable of achieving your goals because it's taking you longer to complete your process than it took others. The problem with these comparisons is that you are entering the first phase of your transformation process and you have no idea what others have experienced, how long it took them to arrive at their present position, or how difficult their process was.

The power of transformation is a spiritual awakening in Christ and an awareness that empowers you to uncover and discover who you were created to be, as you are enlightened and overcome a defeatist mentality.

Everything that you need to be successful is already in you. When you were designed, you were equipped with everything you would need to complete your assignment. A transformed believer (person) with a renewed mind is a death sentence to everything that' opposes their purpose, assignment(s), and destiny. The authority to overcome feelings of inferiority as you uncover and discover who you are and walk-in victory in every area of life is the reality of internal transformation. The enemies of transformation do not want you to know the power of transformation because they don't want you to be informed or transformed; therefore, they attack your sense of value and self-worth in an attempt to hold you hostage. When we understand the transforming power of God, we will be able to comprehend the essence of Jesus's statement when he said; *"I and my Father are One (of the same essence as the Father)."*

> **John 5:30** *I can of my own self do nothing: as I hear, I judge: and my judgement is just; because I seek not mine own will, but the will of the Father which hathe sent me."*

Who have you chosen to be joined to? The overcomer in you; or the defeatist mentality?

Entering a dimension of God that allows Him to impregnate our spirit with His Divine Nature involves spiritual intimacy and trusting Him in a way that transcends the natural, and positions us to see ourselves as God sees us. We are created in His image and likeness, and we have the right to operate with all the delegated authority and power of God as His representative on the Earth. Operating in the capacity of who we are created to be has been a challenge. This is due largely to a religious system and culture that has socialized and modified the church (us) to believe that being united with Christ, and being one spirit with Him is heresy. Being united with Jesus The Anointed is, in fact, the redemptive plan of God to restore the Kingdom of God on Earth and carry out His agenda.

> *Romans 8:17* And if [we are His] children, [then we are His] heirs also: heirs of God and fellow heirs with Christ [sharing His spiritual blessing and inheritance], if indeed we share in His suffering so that we may also share in His glory. (AMP)

Experiencing the transforming power of God allows you to enter a dimension of spiritual awareness wherein you will no longer be ashamed to be recognized as God's offspring while assuming your rightful position as His representative on the Earth. *In Him, you live, move, and have your being.* The thought of oneness with God through Jesus by the power of the Holy Spirit can be paralyzing if you are spiritually and psychologically held hostage by a defeatist mentality, man-made religion, and religious culture.

> *When the light of your internal picture is greater than the darkness of the external picture, you will transform your world.*
> *- Dr. Larry Carnes*

The Law of Reversibility

The Law of Reversibility is a legislated spiritual principle enacted by God that reverses the cultural impact of the kingdom of darkness that entered the Earth through Lucifer. God's counterculture to the kingdom of darkness is the Kingdom of Light.

> **Genesis 1:1** *In the beginning God created the heaven and the earth. 2 And the earth was without form, and void; and darkness was upon the face of the deep. And the Spirit of God moved upon the face of the waters. 3 And God said, Let there be light: and there was light.*

The power of transformation takes the unknown and makes it known by pointing out God's original intent for humanity. It redefines the conditions governing our existence and brings clarity as the law of reversibility becomes operational. *The law of reversibility is a foundational component of the transformation process because it lets us know that* **the spiritual death of humanity from an internal perspective is reversible.** The power of internal spiritual transformation reverses everything from a spiritual perspective that occurred as a result of the decolonization of humanity and the Earth from God's original intent.

> *Oneness with Jesus, The Anointed is, in fact, the redemptive plan of God to restore the Kingdom of God and carry out His agenda on Earth.*

Internal spiritual transformation or inverse transformation is the reproduction or restructuring of your spiritual DNA, which gives birth to who you were created to be initially in the womb of God (the womb of God is God's spirit). Because humanity is created in the image and likeness of God and because we know that God is a Spirit, the fallen state of humanity is spiritually reversible. It's the process by which we are restored to our rightful position. If we are going to be successful in the fulfillment of our Kingdom assignment, we must commit to the process of success and do what successful people do; take action. Spiritual recolonization by way of spiritual transformation, is the pathway to spiritual maturity. It's the Optimum Return to God's original intent.

The law of reversibility is a foundational component of the transformation process because it lets us know that the spiritual death of humanity from an internal perspective is reversible.

Your executive decision to commit to the process of transformation says that you're not willing to remain in a spiritually fallen state. It also says that you will surrender to the process of spiritual transformation and take action to superimpose the will of God.

The spiritual death of humanity is reversible and can be acted out or displayed when we invoke the law of reversibility.

What you decide may seem inconsequential but trust me, it's one of the most significant decisions you will make.

The forgiveness of sin and translation into the Kingdom does not come through behavior modification; it comes through internal spiritual transformation.

Colossians 1:9 For this reason we also, from the day we heard of it, have not ceased to pray and make special] request for you, [asking] that you may be filled with the full (deep and clear) knowledge of His will in all spiritual wisdom in comprehensive insight into the ways and purposes of God] and in understanding and discernment of spiritual things 10 That you may walk (live and conduct yourselves) in a manner worthy of the Lord, fully pleasing to Him and desiring to please Him in all things, bearing fruit in every good work and steadily growing and increasing in and by the knowledge of God [with fuller, deeper, and clearer insight, acquaintance, and recognition]. 11 [We pray] that you may be invigorated and strengthened with all power according to the might of His glory, [to exercise] every kind of endurance and patience (perseverance and forbearance) with joy, 12 Giving thanks to the Father, Who has qualified and made us fit to share the portion which is the inheritance of the saints (God's holy

*people) in the Light. 13 [The Father] has delivered and drawn us
to Himself out of the control and the dominion of darkness and
has transferred us into the kingdom of the Son of His love, 14 In
Whom we have our redemption through His blood, [which means]
the forgiveness of our sins. 15 [Now] He is the exact likeness of the
unseen God [the visible representation of the invisible]; He is the
Firstborn of all creation. (AMP)*

*I John 4:12 No man has at any time [yet] seen God. But if we love
one another, God abides (lives and remains) in us and His love
(that love which is essentially His) is brought to completion (to its
full maturity, runs its full course, is perfected) in us! 13 By this we
come to know (perceive, recognize, and understand) that we abide
(live and remain) in Him and He in us: because He has given
(imparted) to us of His [Holy] Spirit. 14 And [besides] we ourselves
have seen (have deliberately and steadfastly contemplated) and
bear witness that the Father has sent the Son [as the] Savior of the
world. 15 Anyone who confesses (acknowledges, owns) that Jesus is
the Son of God, God abides (lives, makes His home) in him and he
[abides, lives, makes his home] in God. 16 And we know
(understand, recognize, are conscious of, by observation and by
experience) and believe (adhere to and put faith in and rely on) the
love God cherishes for us. God is love, and he who dwells and
continues in love dwells and continues in God, and God dwells
and continues in him. 17 In this [union and communion with
Him] love is brought to completion and attains perfection with us,
that we may have confidence for the day of judgment [with
assurance and boldness to face Him], because as He is, so are we in
this world. (AMPC)*

Confession

*I am filled with the full deep and clear knowledge of God's will in all
spiritual wisdom, and I walk, live, and conduct myself in a manner worthy of*

the Lord. God has delivered and drawn me to Him, out of the control and the dominion of darkness, and has transferred me into the Kingdom of the Son of His love. I am redeemed by the blood of Jesus.

Transformation Requires Self-Knowledge

Self-Knowledge may be the most critical component of your transformational process. When asked, "who are you?" How do you answer? Do you know who you are, or, are you playing the hand that your decisions and experiences have dealt you? How willing are you to be honest with yourself and remove the mask of deception to reveal what lies beneath your surface?

On a scale of zero to ten, with ten being the highest (very willing), how willing are you, to be vulnerable, honest, and transparent with yourself, so that you can escape the limitations that have been established in your mind, released into your spirit, and caused you to be self-institutionalized? Where would you honestly place yourself? Are you a five or below, or, do you see yourself as a six or above? Have you deceived yourself and others about things that took place in your life for so long that your deception has become your truth? Is it holding you hostage and causing you to have a false perception of who you are?

Vulnerability and Honesty Scale
0 1 2 3 4 5 6 7 8 9 10

Being authentic is being honest, credible, genuine, and not false in your beliefs or actions.

If you want to discover who you are and escape the false beliefs of being better than; or inferior to, you must be willing to dig deeper, and ask how well you know your true self? This is not based on your physical appearance or the image that you project for others, but the real you; with all your talents, motivations, and flaws. Self-knowledge is the foundation for transformation because if we refuse to acknowledge and accept the truth of who we have become, we will refuse to rise and manifest the person we were created to be.

It's been said that knowledge is power. I want to extend that to say that knowledge is power only if you apply and use that which you are knowledgeable of; because knowledge without application leads to disappointment and frustration.

> *"Power without the Passion of Christ becomes abuse.*
> *Dr. Larry Carnes*

2Peter 1:1 From Simon Peter, a servant and apostle of Jesus Christ To those who have obtained a faith that is as valuable as ours, a faith based on the approval that comes from our God and Savior, Jesus Christ. 2 May good will[a] and peace fill your lives through your knowledge about Jesus, our God and Lord! 3 God's divine power has given us everything we need for life and for godliness. This power was given to us through knowledge of the one who called us by his own glory and integrity. 4 Through his glory and integrity, he has given us his promises that are of the highest value. Through these promises, you will share in the divine nature because you have escaped the corruption that sinful desires cause in the world. 5 Because of this, make every effort to add integrity to your faith; and to integrity add knowledge; (GW)

Your empowerment journey to discover who you are at the deepest level starts with knowing yourself.

Understanding and becoming knowledgeable of your purpose, gifts, and passion will assist you as you gain the confidence to establish the relationships that complement who you are; and set goals that are achievable but stretch you to extend beyond your comfort zone.

REFLECTION: Start your empowerment and the transformational journey by asking yourself: What are you most motivated to discover about yourself?

Being Knowledgeable of Your Strength to Endure

Every person who succeeds in life does so by persevering in the face of adversity and by continually applying themselves to their vision. No one comes to this Earth with talents and abilities that are fully functional. Instead, they dedicate years of their life to discovering who they are and developing their skills. You must be unwilling to let setbacks or failures determine your destiny. Choose, instead, to step forward every time you experience a setback.

God has given you amazing gifts, gifts that you may be aware of and some you have yet to discover. It's time to stop minimizing your potential through comparison and imagine the extraordinary possibilities of all that you can be!

Transformation is an Internal Spiritual Investment!

The Power of Awareness

The Power of Awareness deals with the duality of consciousness involving your conscious and unconscious state. When you are aware of Whose you are, you become aware of who you are. When the I Am within you is awakened, the power of awareness will foster internal illumination as you discover who you were created to be. Your conscience is what you know. Your subconscious is who you are. To be spiritually unconscious is to be unaware of who you were created to be. Spiritual Intelligence is key to internal spiritual illumination because it involves knowing God and making Him known. When you become aware of Who God is, you will be awakened to who you are in Him.

1 John 4:4 My dear children, you come from God and belong to God. You have already won a big victory over those false teachers, for the Spirit in you is far stronger than anything in the world. (MSG)

Ephesians 4:16 May He grant you out of the riches of His glory, to be strengthened and spiritually energized with power through His Spirit in your inner self, [indwelling your innermost being and personality], 17 so that Christ may dwell in your hearts through your faith. And may you, having been [deeply] rooted and [securely] grounded in love, 18 be fully capable of comprehending with all the saints (God's people) the width and length and height and depth of His love [fully experiencing that amazing, endless love]; 19 and [that you may come] to know [practically, through personal experience] the love of Christ which far surpasses [mere] knowledge [without experience], that you may be filled up [throughout your being] to all the fullness of God [so that you may have the richest experience of God's presence in your lives, completely filled and flooded with God Himself]. (AMP)

Your Eschatology "Life's Assignment"

Jesus's conception does not make sense. When looked at from a natural perspective, it can't be explained. His birth, death, and resurrection, however, were a part of His eschatology (life's assignment) that was ordained before the foundation of the earth.

Isaiah 6:6 For to us a Child shall be born, to us a Son shall be given; And the government shall be upon His shoulder, And His name shall be called Wonderful Counselor, Mighty God, Everlasting Father, Prince of Peace. 7 There shall be no end to the increase of His government and of peace, [He shall rule] on the throne of David and over his kingdom, To establish it and to uphold it with justice and righteousness From that time forward and

> *forevermore. The zeal of the Lord of hosts will accomplish*
> *this. (AMP)*

> **1 Peter 1:18** *Forasmuch as ye know that ye were not redeemed with*
> *corruptible things, as silver and gold, from your vain conversation*
> *received by tradition from your fathers; 19 But with the precious*
> *blood of Christ, as of a lamb without blemish and without spot: 20*
> *Who verily was foreordained before the foundation of the world,*
> *but was manifest in these last times for you,*

> **Revelation 13:8** *And all that dwell upon the earth shall worship him,*
> *whose names are not written in the book of life of the Lamb slain*
> *from the foundation of the world.*

Jesus's assignment was determined before he appeared physically. The writers of **Psalms 40:6-8**, and, **Hebrews 10:5-7** recorded it. Jesus says... **Hebrews 10:7** *"Behold, I have come To do Your will, O God [To fulfill] what is written of Me in the scroll of the book."* (AMP)

Just like Jesus, you were ordained by God before the foundation of the Earth for a specific reason. The circumstances by which you arrived did not take God by surprise because God is all-knowing. Therefore, the fall of humanity and the consequences of Adams disobedience did not negate the purpose and plan of God for your life. Your eschatology; (life's assignment) was determined and designed by God before the foundation of the world. The dichotomy (contradictory differences) of being who you were created to be and the reality of who you are is determined by your willingness to submit to the process of transformation and the Law of Becoming.

> **Eph. 1:4** *According as he hath chosen us in him before the foundation*
> *of the world, that we should be holy and without blame before him*
> *in love: 5 Having predestinated us unto the adoption of children*
> *by Jesus Christ to himself, according to the good pleasure of his*
> *will,*

__Eph. 2:10__ For we are His workmanship [His own master work, a work of art], created in Christ Jesus [reborn from above— spiritually transformed, renewed, ready to be used] for good works, which God prepared [for us] beforehand [taking paths which He set], so that we would walk in them [living the good life which He prearranged and made ready for us]. (AMP)

Confession

Because I know Whose I am, I know who I am. When I received God's Son, I became God's son.

Confession

Because I am begotten by the Begotten of God, I am the begotten of God. Therefore, I am of God and have overcome. Because He that's in me is greater, I am awakened to my Godself.

REFLECTION: Briefly describe what you discovered about yourself and where you are in your transformational journey.

TRANSFORMATIONAL POINTS

1. Everything that you need to be successful is in you. You were designed and equipped with everything needed to complete your assignment.
2. A transformed believer (person) with a renewed mind is a death sentence to everything that's opposed to their purpose, assignment(s), and destiny.
3. The law of reversibility is a foundational component of the transformation process because it lets us know that "the spiritual death of humanity from an internal perspective is reversible."
4. To discover who you are and escape the false beliefs of being better than; or inferior to, you must be willing to dig deeper and ask; how well do you know your true self?
5. The Power of Awareness deals with the duality of consciousness involving your conscious and unconscious state. When you are aware of Whose you are, you become aware of who you are.
6. Spiritual recolonization by way of spiritual transformation is the pathway to spiritual maturity. It's the Optimum Return to God's original intent.

2

HOLY SPIRIT: THE AGENT OF TRANSFORMATION

The possibility of transformation without the active involvement of the Holy Spirit is an unrealistic expectation. He (Holy Spirit) is the initiator of transformation. He's the quickening agent who empowers and transforms the spirit of your mind as you are enlightened through the process of spiritual illumination. It's through this process of spiritual enlightenment that your inner healing takes place and you enjoy a recreated spirit. The Holy Spirit initiates our capacity to be spiritually sensitive and recognizes the need to position ourselves for the process of transformation to start.

> **Matthew 3:16** *And Jesus, when he was baptized, went up straightway out of the water: and, lo, the heavens were opened unto him, and he saw the Spirit of God descending like a dove, and lighting upon him: 17 And lo a voice from heaven, saying, This is my beloved Son, in whom I am well pleased.*

It was the transforming power of the Holy Spirit that empowered Jesus to become the Christ, the Anointed One. The power of the Holy Spirit recreates our internal spirit and comes to indwell in us immediately upon salvation. His work within us, however, takes a lifetime. His job is to empower us to do everything that God desires and to transform us into who we are created to be.

> **Matthew 3:11** *I indeed baptize you with water unto repentance. but he that cometh after me is mightier than I, whose shoes I am not worthy to bear: he shall baptize you with the Holy Ghost, and with fire:*

> **Romans 8:1** *Therefore there is now no condemnation [no guilty verdict, no punishment] for those who are in Christ Jesus [who believe in Him as personal Lord and Savior]. 2 For the law of the Spirit of life [which is] in Christ Jesus [the law of our new being] has set you free from the law of sin and of death. 3 For what the Law could not do [that is, overcome sin and remove its penalty, its power] being weakened by the flesh [man's nature without the Holy Spirit], God did: He sent His own Son in the likeness of sinful man as an offering for sin. And He condemned sin in the flesh [subdued it and overcame it in the person of His own Son], 4 so that the [righteous and just] requirement of the Law might be fulfilled in us who do not live our lives in the ways of the flesh [guided by worldliness and our sinful nature], but [live our lives] in the ways of the Spirit [guided by His power]. (AMP)*

We have a constant Helper who reminds us of who we are in Christ and empowers us to overcome the challenges of life. We depend on the power of the Holy Spirit. Knowing that we have a Helper does not mean that we will not have difficulties, conflicts, or misunderstandings; instead, it means that He guards our paths and gives us His wisdom as we navigate the journey of life. The internal restructuring of your spiritual DNA; (recreated spirit), is the work of the Holy Spirit. He is the initiator of internal spiritual transformation.

The Law of Brokenness

Embracing your authentic self and understanding how God has empowered you are the first steps toward transformation and living in divine authority. The authentic you is created in the image and likeness of God; the modified you became a servant of self-gratification due to the failed actions of humanity. Therefore, it stands to reason that the natural inclination of the fallen nature is to cater to the delicacies of the flesh. These delicacies are the areas in life where we find ourselves being challenged by the enemies of the Kingdom. The divine nature of God in you is challenged by the fallen nature of humanity. The fallen nature of humanity is the enemy of spiritual transformation. Its first objective is to entice you in areas that cater to self-gratification. The lust of the flesh, the lust of the eye, and the pride of life are the targeted areas. Our willingness to resist these challenges and submit to the will of God is a choice. God does not break us or force us to obey. We choose brokenness by surrendering to God and His Kingdom; which is the sovereignty of God, His divine authority over evil forces, and His governmental rule. Here's the proposition: "If you are willing and obedient."

Natural wisdom may be knowing yourself, but fearing God is the beginning of spiritual wisdom!

Matt. 26:38 *Then saith he unto them, My soul is exceeding sorrowful, even unto death: tarry ye here, and watch with me. 39 And he went a little farther, and fell on his face, and prayed, saying, O my Father, if it be possible, let this cup pass from me: nevertheless not as I will, but as thou wilt. 40 And he cometh unto the disciples, and findeth them asleep, and saith unto Peter, What, could ye not watch with me one hour? 41 Watch and pray, that ye enter not into temptation: the spirit indeed is willing, but the flesh is weak. 42 He went away again the second time, and prayed, saying, O my Father, if this cup may not pass away from me, except I drink it, thy will be done.*

Choosing to be broken before God can be an easy choice, but it is not necessarily an easy process even when we are empowered and transformed by the Holy Spirit. He, Holy Spirit, is the Agent of Transformation. Spiritual transformation cannot happen without the personal intimacy and involvement of the Holy Spirit. I believe that the only way to cultivate an intimate relationship with the Holy Spirit is to spend time communicating with Him and praying in the spirit (praying in your spiritual prayer language). It's during these personal and intimate times of fellowship with the Holy Spirit that we are encouraged and build our most holy faith. It's during these times that there is an inner communication taking place that cannot be understood by the natural man because we are connecting with God in the Spirit, our original tongue.

> *Jude 1:20 But you, beloved, build yourselves up on [the foundation of your most holy faith [continually progress, rise like an edifice higher and higher], pray in the Holy Spirit, (AMP)*

The divine nature of God in you is challenged by the fallen nature of humanity.

Brokenness and surrendering to the process of transformation is incomprehensible if you have not surrendered your will and submitted to the transforming power of the Holy Spirit. Surrendering to a purpose or cause requires an unconditional commitment to the cause and an understanding of the depth to which one must surrender to God. To surrender is to stop resisting by yielding to the authority. Surrendering to the Holy Spirit is the first step in the process of transformation.

Recolonization of Humanity and the Earth to God

Colonization is the establishment of governmental authority, rule, and culture in a distant domain; it's the extension of a king's influence. Recolonization is the act of re-establishing the king's governmental authority, influence, rule, and culture after it has been interrupted.

The Holy Spirit is the administrator of the recolonization of humanity and the Earth back to God. The recolonization of humanity to God is accomplished through the Holy Spirit as recorded in the first chapter of Genesis when the Earth was without form and void. Humanity's spiritual separation from God took place because of the actions of Adam. His actions caused humanity to decolonize (spiritually separate) from God and His Kingdom. The absence of the governmental authority and rule of God in the life of humanity caused them to wallow in ignorance and become spiritually void and dark.

> **Genesis 1:26** *Then God said, "Let us make humankind in our image, in the likeness of ourselves; and let them rule over the fish in the sea, the birds in the air, the animals, and over all the earth, and over every crawling creature that crawls on the earth." 27 So God created humankind in his own image; in the image of God he created him: male and female he created them. 28 God blessed them: God said to them, "Be fruitful, multiply, fill the earth and subdue it. Rule over the fish in the sea, the birds in the air and every living creature that crawls on the earth." (CJB)*

The spiritual recolonization of humanity to God is accomplished by the transforming power of the Holy Spirit.

In his book, *Empty Temple: The Neglected Holy Spirit*, Archbishop Kirby Clements states: *"the Holy Spirit is the dispenser of 'Common Grace'* (**Matt. 5:45, Luke 6:35**). *"Common Grace is that general operation of the Holy Spirit whereby He, without renewing the heart, exercises such a moral influence on humanity that sin is restrained and order is maintained in social life so that God's purposes are realized."*

> **Genesis 3:9** *And the LORD God called unto Adam, and said unto him,*

Where art thou? 10 And he said, I heard thy voice in the garden, and I was afraid, because I was naked; and I hid myself. 11 And he said, Who told thee that thou was naked? Hast thou eaten of the tree, whereof I commanded thee that thou shouldest not eat?

Colonization through habitation. God inhabits us through His presence in us, through the Holy Spirit.

The decision to decolonize and spiritually separate from God was an act of humanity's will, and God never violates a person's will. The proposition is *"if you be willing and obedient."* The Law of the Will involves willingly surrendering to God through submission, not force. When we have the option to do or not to do, we reserve the right to exercise our free will to accept or reject the Gift of Life and step back into the Father through Jesus by the power of the Holy Spirit.

Proverbs 1:23 "If you will turn and pay attention to my rebuke, Behold, I [Wisdom] will pour out my spirit on you; I will make my words known to you. (AMP)

Revelation 2:16 So return to me and change the way you think and act, or I will come to you quickly and wage war against them with the sword from my mouth. (GWT)

The Optimum Return is what God said to me years ago during what can best be described as my entrance into the painful process of transformation by way of exile. I use the word exiled because I heard these words, *"Why sit here and die?"* I felt exiled because I was no longer a part of a ministry that I had been connected to for seventeen years. I found myself having to willingly decolonize from a place of stagnation and darkness; so that I could recolonize through my painful process of internal spiritual transformation. I had to willingly go into exile, into the wilderness, on the backside of the mountain.

The choice was mine. I could be sensitive to the Voice of God and the unction of the Holy Spirit, or I could sit there and die. God did not force me to leave Augusta, GA. He simply asked me a question. *"Why sit here and die?"* I choose to turn aside to see, listen , respond, and take action. There was a necessary ending that needed to take place in my life. The brook in Augusta, GA had dried up. It was another phase in my transformational process. It was time to go out on a limb, spin my cocoon, and begin the process of being dependent on God. I entered my place of internal isolation and started my wilderness experience while the world around me looked on, but I had no idea of how intense the internal battle would be to ward off depression, a sense of failure, and a defeatist mentality. If I was going to survive, I would have to depend on the person and power of the Holy Spirit and bring an end to my defeatist mentality.

REFLECTION: Why are you reluctant to bring necessary endings to things in your life that have dried up? Are you so co-dependent that you are holding on to what's rejected you because you think it's your lifeline?

Your burning bush will not appear until you are in the right place, in the right season.

REFLECTION: Describe a time in your journey when you felt abandoned and forced into exile. Now, I want you to reflect on it and decide if it was spiritual, relational, emotional, or psychological darkness that you found yourself battling.

When the Kingdom of God which is the Kingdom of Light, penetrates darkness, darkness cannot remain, it has no authority in the matter, so it must go. The presence of the Holy Spirit is liberating because He has the power to eradicate darkness and set the atmosphere for God to speak. The Spirit that breaks the power of darkness and initiates spiritual illumination is the Agent of Enlightenment, the Holy Spirit. I must caution you, however, and bring your attention to the fact that darkness will not leave voluntarily; you have to take authority over darkness. I hear your question; "How do I take authority over darkness?" You take authority over darkness by giving place to the Word of God, declaring it over your situation, and allowing it to adjudicate on your behalf.

> **Genesis 1:1** *In the beginning God created the heaven and the earth. 2 And the earth was without form, and void; and darkness was upon the face of the deep. And the Spirit of God moved upon the face of the waters. 3 And God said, Let there be light: and there was light.*

How would you respond if asked the following questions by the King of kings? *"Will you trust Me to be your Creator, your Redeemer, and your Guide? Am I God enough to you that you will trust me to be Who I say I Am, and to do what I say I will do? Or have you made Me too small in your life and elevated your situations above My Word and commitment to perform my Word? Will you trust Me?*

REFLECTION: **Meditate and reflect on the questions above, and give serious thought to them before you respond.**

REFLECTION: **Now, take the time to think about your reply. Was it from the conceptual or experiential point of view?**

The Spirit of The Breaker

A breaker is someone or something used for opening or closing a circuit. A breakthrough is an offensive thrust that penetrates and carries beyond a defensive barrier. The Messiah, the One who breaks open the way, leads you and restores all that pertains to the promises of God.

> **Micah 1:13** *"The [a]breaker [the Messiah, who opens the way] shall go up before them [liberating them].They will break out, pass through the gate and go out;So their King goes on before them,The Lord at their head." (AMP)*

The principles of God don't divide the world into sacred versus secular or religious versus political. Life is integrated; That's why the Word of God declares that *"it rains on the just and the unjust."(Matt. 5:45)* The Words of God have a powerful meaning. Jesus's words suggest that His "good news" describe a powerful transformation that rescues people.

1. The Spirit of the Breaker gives you Victory. **Micah 1:13**
2. God's Word is a Breaker. **Matt. 4:4, Heb.4:12**
3. The Blood of Jesus is a Breaker. **Revelation 12:11a**
4. Prayer and Praise are Breakers. **Acts 12:5**

The Spirit of the Breaker is the light of God shining upon you and removing everything that's had you chained spiritually, psychologically, emotionally, and relationally. The chains have fallen off that once held you captive. Once the chains that held your mind captive, chains of low self-esteem, chains of fear, failure, poverty, and chains of sickness are removed, you are free.

> **Joel 2:28** *And it shall come to pass afterward, that I will pour out my spirit upon all flesh; and your sons and your daughters shall prophesy, your old men shall dream dreams, your young men shall see visions:*

When you let the Spirit of Light shine from within you, you will escape the darkness of spiritual, psychological, and emotional hell.

Dr. Larry Carnes

The recolonization of humanity back to God is a spiritual emancipation that's initiated by the Holy Spirit; He is the Spirit of Liberty and Truth. We don't have to depend on our human reasoning; we have a supernatural guide in the form of God's indwelling Holy Spirit. Give place to the Holy Spirit in your life and enjoy spiritual emancipation as you are empowered and transformed from the inside out.

The power of transformation is choosing to escape from the emotional and psychological terrorist of your past and present in order to enjoy the freedom and victory of your Now!

REFLECTION: As you reflect upon this chapter, capture some key points that stood out to you that you may agree or disagree with, and share the impact that they will have during a group discussion.

WHY

Why?
Why do I cry and feel like a clown? I bring smiles to the hearts of others but inside, it's dark and I drown. Why?
Why do I perform to make others laugh, while living in internal darkness and experiencing emotional hell? Why?
I'm with you in the natural, or so it may appear, but in my spirit, I drift into darkness and drown in my tears.
In my attempt to escape the pain of unrealistic expectations, I drift further into darkness; I need spiritual emancipation.
Empowered by the Spirit and Image that I'm created in, I refuse to remain an emotional hostage. I'll escape the cell that I've been living in.
Empowered by the Holy Spirit, I decided to break free. The power was in me all the time. The Holy Spirit has transformed me.
Why?
Larry Carnes

TRANSFORMATIONAL POINTS

1. The possibility of transformation without the active involvement of the Holy Spirit is an unrealistic expectation. He (Holy Spirit) is the initiator of transformation.
2. It was the transforming power of the Holy Spirit that empowered Jesus to become the Christ, the Anointed One.
3. The power of the Holy Spirit recreates our internal spirit and comes to dwell in us immediately upon salvation.
4. It's the divine nature of God in you that the enemy challenges.
5. The presence of the Holy Spirit is liberating because He has the power to eradicate darkness and set the atmosphere for God to speak.

IDENTIFYING THE ENEMIES OF TRANSFORMATION

U nrealistic expectations can be a death sentence to the fulfillment of your purpose and destiny. Because we live in a performance-driven society, we tend to place value on the opinion of others and what they think of us. *One of the biggest lies of life is: "My performance plus the opinion of others equal my self-worth."* The key to overcoming this value based on performance mentality is identifying and acknowledging its existence and taking the necessary steps to eliminate it.

REFLECTION: Have you sentenced yourself to transformational death because of the pressure to compare your process with someone else's? If so, briefly describe.

Are your expectations of yourself realistic, or have you imposed unrealistic expectations upon yourself?

The Enemies (Barriers) of Transformation

Two enemies stand in the path of transformation. Your failure to identify and address them could result in long-term, unresolved issues. These two enemies are internal and external barriers. Our strategies for not only identifying but addressing these barriers will determine our success or failure in overcoming them. The enemies in our lives aren't always spiritual; they can be physical, psychological, and emotional. Properly identifying, categorizing, addressing, and developing a strategy to overcome these enemies is critical for a successful transformation.

A barrier can be defined as something that blocks or is intended to block a passage. When people pursue goals, they face barriers that are both visible and invisible. The key to properly developing a successful strategy for transformation is to understand the types of barriers you will face as you strive to reach your personal goals, and ultimately your destiny. With this knowledge, you can consider which barriers are most problematic in your life and deal with them accordingly.

We must know the difference between barriers that are meant to protect us from harmful situations or conditions, and those that are trying to keep us from reaching our desired destination or goal.

External Enemies (Barriers)

People, places, and things are external but can affect you internally if given the opportunity. These external enemies to transformation are easy to identify and address because they exist above the surface. The challenge that comes up while dealing with and eliminating them is an issue of soul ties and codependency. Because we are relational beings and have a need to be in a relationship with others, we may, at times, depend on outside relationships to determine our value and significance. As you navigate your path to transformation some of your greatest challenges may be dealing with the people factor and how these relationships impact your life.

The ability to adequately, successfully, and humbly eliminate unhealthy relationships with people, places, and things may be challenging to start with, but it's necessary and must be done promptly. It's important to understand the need for *necessary endings* in life. All relationships are not meant to last a lifetime; there are, in fact, some relationships that we should have never entered. And by the way, that includes some marriages!

The *first step* in dealing with barriers is to give them a name and realize the role they play in blocking progress. External distractions include factors such as visual triggers, social interactions, text messages, and phone calls. The *next key* is the acknowledgment that the barrier exists. Self-denial and the unwillingness to be honest with yourself can be the number one hindrance to your success in eliminating the barriers to transformation in your life. The *third key* is to take action. Identifying and acknowledging the barriers without taking the necessary actions to eliminate those barriers is the same as having an umbrella and refusing to use it when it's raining, while complaining about getting wet.

David had to distance himself from Saul, his family, home, friend, and position to bring a *necessary ending to a toxic external relationship that became an internal enemy.* David's connection to Saul had become so stressful that it caused emotional and psychological barriers to surface in his life. These emotional and psychological pressures gave birth to fear and caused him to modify his behavior (*1Sam. 21:11-13*).

REFLECTION: Identify the external enemies that are barriers to your internal transformation, and design a plan to eliminate them from your life.

When considering relationships that we need to end, we seldom consider ending the ones that feed our EGO. Relationships that feed your EGO may be an enemy to your transformation!

Internal Enemies (Barriers)

When we speak of the most challenging and intimidating enemies of transformation we are speaking from an internal perspective and not referring to the external. The greatest enemies that you will face and must overcome individually are not external but internal. These enemies are difficult to recognize because they hide beneath the surface of who we are. In essence, because of internal damages, and our refusal to be honest with ourselves by addressing our toxic behaviors; we camouflage our greatest enemies in an attempt to be who we are expected to be because we are afraid to let the world see who we are.

One of the most fascinating things to me is how professionals who are in the business of helping others overcome relational, emotional, psychological, and other challenges that they are facing in life; are so close to the forest that they can't see the trees (barriers) in their lives. I've seen them get defensive and talk over others when someone voices an opinion that's different from theirs. I've seen how adamant they are in defending their opinion. The interesting thing about their behavior is that they are very effective at what they do, and have helped hundreds overcome the internal barriers in their lives.

My question is, what inner healing needs to take place in them that they are blind to because they are so busy analyzing and trying to assist others?

REFLECTION: My questions for you are, does inner healing need to take place before we can help others? And, does analyzing and trying to assist others become an internal barrier to our transformation?

Are you letting the little foxes of your past spoil your vine, hold you hostage, and keep you from living a fulfilled and happy life? Are you a victim of self-defeating thoughts? Self-defeating thoughts are the memories of the negative experiences, words, or actions that you rehearse from your past and have been given access to your now. Unfortunately, these self-defeating thoughts have become the norm for so many people that they appear automatically. They have become their norms, standards, and beliefs!

Internal enemies (barriers) to transformation can come in the form of guilt, false beliefs, shame, self-pity, co-dependency, blame, and a superiority complex to name a few. Feelings of being insignificant and unvalued are major contributors to the totality of a person's perspective of who they are. These feelings may lead to habitually destructive behaviors. As you can see, the battle to identify and overcome internal barriers can be complicated with the assistance of the Holy Spirit (Agent of Transformation). Imagine the difficulties of trying to overcome these potential enemies without the Agent of Transformation.

REFLECTION: Looking at the list of the potential internal enemies listed above, identify three that you've encountered, and briefly describe how you were impacted.

Self-Perception

The first step to overcoming internal barriers is to transform your perception of who you are. It's unfortunate, but many times, our perception of who we are is based on the way others see us and who they perceive us to be. Take a moment to think about the mental tapes that are stored in your memory bank, which is your emotional and psychological hard drive. When you replay the tapes, what do you hear? Are they gratifying and encouraging, or do they hunt you from a negative perspective and tear you down? If allowed, they can, and will become the internal terrorist that taunts you, holds you hostage, and, over time, causes you to emotionally and psychologically institutionalize yourself. I call it "self-imposed institutionalization."

What tapes are you replaying that create the world in which you live? Do they foster automatic negative thoughts that tear you down and cause you to think less of yourself? Or, are you fostering performance-enhancing thoughts that edify, empower, and build you up to believe that you are capable of achieving all that you set your mind to do? What's your perception of who you are?

Transforming Self-Perception Through Internal Visualization

"If you can visualize it, you can materialize it." Dr. Larry Carnes

The following statement is one that I've said to myself and others throughout the years, Little did I know during its conception how important it would become to me personally and how I would need to say it over and over to resist the temptation to quit when it looked like none of the promises of God for my life were coming to pass. As I experienced feelings of shame, defeat, embarrassment, rejection, insignificance, and being unappreciated, and, at times, worthlessness, I had to stand before the people of God and declare the message of the Kingdom that I truly believed with all my heart. But on the inside, I was in a dark place and believed no one cared. So I asked the question, "What about me?"

"The promises of God are greater than your challenges."

As I have strived to complete this mandated assignment from God, I've faced great challenges and experienced some major relational, financial, and material losses. My challenge and yours is to control our thoughts and emotions (feelings) during these challenging times and to take authority over the self-defeating mindset that says, Here we go again, it's never going to come to pass. If we are not mindful of the faithfulness of God, and if we allow ourselves to be consumed by the challenges of life, we will fall victim to the ghosts of our pasts and start to listen to the old tapes of the negative things that were said to us.

It's time to forget the things that are behind us. Clear your memory bank of the negative messages, and reboot!

I am visualizing myself as I want to be and *speaking life* to what I see in my spirit. One of the resources that I use is a vision board that has pictures of my dreams and aspirations on it. The board has pictures of the flags of countries that I've said I would travel to. There are pictures of me standing before people ministering, affirmations, pictures of the homes, and cars, and, yes, the vacation spots that I want to go to are on the board too.

Because God is total Spirit, He Saw, Said, and Released from Himself, what He Declared with His Mouth.

> *Genesis 1:2 And the earth was without form, and void; and darkness was upon the face of the deep. And the Spirit of God moved upon the face of the waters. 3 And God said, Let there be light: and there was light.*

As difficult as it may be for you to imagine and picture God the Creator being surrounded by something other than what He desired, He spoke life to what He wanted and transformed the world! God is so transparent that He allows us to witness the many challenges that He faced as the Almighty God. What challenges could God have, you may ask? Let's start with this truth, *God is Omniscient (all-knowing, all-wise, all-seeing); therefore, nothing takes Him by surprise.*

The rebellion of Lucifer *(Is. 14:12, Ez. 28:14);* and the disobedience and spiritual fall of Adam and Eve *(Gen. 3:6)* did not take God by surprise. But as you can see, there were challenges to God's original plan. The strategy that God used to transform darkness into light is the strategy of the Kingdom, and it's the same strategy that will transform your world. The strategy of the Kingdom is the **Sovereign Governmental Rule and Authority of God.**

God is Sovereign. He's The Supreme Ruler. What is God's perception of Himself? "I Am" (Ex. 3:14)! He's consistent and greater than any situation that He may face (**Heb. 6:3, Ja. 1:17**).

Jesus Visualized and Declared His Victory

I love Jesus's talk with His Father in **John 17.** Jesus' request is to experience the Optimum Return and be *"glorified with God in the same way that He was before the world was."* When I saw this years ago in **John 17:11**; I realized that spiritually Jesus had gained the victory over what He was going to face in the natural. His statement was; *"And now I am no more in the world, but these are in the world, and I come to thee."* It's an indication of His ability to escape the limitations of His sensory perception (limitations of the senses). When I received the revelation from this statement, it blew my mind. It speaks volumes because it says that Jesus is aware of who He is; He had gained the victory over the garden, the betrayal, Pilate's court, and the cross; although He had to experience them in the natural. In essence, Jesus was saying; "I've gained the victory; I'm already gone and seated at the right hand of the Father."

I've taught this principle on several occasions for twenty-five years while ministering in a South Carolina Correctional Facility. It has become one of the staples of faith that I use to demonstrate to the inmates that their natural situations are not too big for God and that internal spiritual freedom is obtainable during their incarceration. During the meetings, I would ask; "When is your release date?" Their response was, "I'm already gone!" There have been several testimonies of releases, and one was so unexpected that I received a call from the facility informing me that an inmate who was not up for parole that I gave a prophetic word of knowledge to had been released. The power of internal transformation and visualization birthed the external manifestation. That's not to say that we are reintroducing the name it and claim it move that was so popular years ago. It does, however, speak to the degree that we trust God and have faith in Him and His divine will. Because we trust God and have faith in Him. we are not limited to our sensory perception.

Speak to your situation and declare the purpose of God for your life.

Jesus's process was filled with painful challenges that included the feeling of being forsaken. He asked God, *"Why hast thou forsaken me?"* *(Matt. 27:46)* The truth of the matter is that Jesus knew that God would never leave or forsake Him, but this part of His process was painful to the degree that He felt alone and abandoned because of the separation from the Father that He would experience. His perception, however, of how He saw Himself, as recorded in *John 17*, was greater than the realities of His situation, but He still had to go through the painful process.

Your process of transformation will have challenges; The question is, will you react or respond to the challenges? Your course of action determines your success or failure. After having an opportunity to peek into parts of Jesus's transformational process, are you sure that you want to submit to the internal process of spiritual transformation? If so, are you willing to visualize and speak life into what you want? What I'm speaking of is not a "name it and claim it" mentality. I'm speaking of standing on the Word of God by faith, and believing that God's will for your life will come to pass.

On the transformation scale of zero to ten, with ten being the highest, where are you on your transformational journey; and what is your perception of who you are? Be honest with yourself. Is there a possibility that you may not be as high on that scale as you think you are? After years of being in my transformational process, based on my response to recent events, I've discovered that I'm not where I thought I was.

Where are you on the scale of internal transformation?
0 1 2 3 4 5 6 7 8 9 10

The Formula for Transformation

Think It – Self-Perception. Transform your thinking, transform your world. (**Prov. 23:7**)

See It – The ability to visualize, and look beyond pre-existing conditions. (2 Cor. 5:7)

Understand It – Being knowledgeable of seasons and timing. Process! (Eccl. 3:1)

Speak It – The declaration of the desired thing. Make positive affirmations. (Job 22:28)

Be It – Demonstrative actions that correspond with your affirmations. (James 2:24)

Make this confession:

I am greater than my situations because my self-worth is in who God created me to be, not in who others expect me to be. I am greatness personified!

The Power to Transform Your I- Factor

In his book, The I-Factor, Dr. Van Moody addresses issues related to everyday life and how people think about themselves, feel about themselves, and relate to themselves. Dr. Moody wrights, *"Your I-Factor is a combination of the dynamics that converge to form the totality of your relationship with you. It's more than self-worth or self-respect. It goes beyond matters of character and motives. It reaches pasts a sense of significance or perception of purpose. It does include relational skills with other people, but most importantly, your I-Factor has everything to do with your relationship with yourself. It's about managing yourself and your life well."*

One of the unfortunate realities of the I-Factor is that unhealthy people think they are healthy, like who they are, and have convinced themselves that they are all right.

Adolf Hitler is a classic example of someone with a distorted view of a healthy I-Factor. What makes it worse is that they surrounded themselves with people who feed their I-Factor dysfunctions. The power of your relationship with yourself has two faces; and, it can be the most dangerous relationship you will ever have or the most awesome and rewarding relationship that you will ever have.

Your internal relationship with yourself is the difference maker between success and failure. No one can derail your destiny as quickly or effectively as you can.

You, however, can also position yourself for success and the fulfillment of your dreams. No one has the authority to do it for you. Titles and positions do not add to your value and self-worth or make you successful. If titles and positions are major factors in determining your value and self-worth, you have a distorted perception of your significance and who you are.

Winning the internal battle and taking control of your mind, will, and emotions are key to having a healthy I-Factor and requires to some degree, an understanding of three dynamics:

- *Your Identity:* When you understand your identity, you know who you are. Knowing who you are is the foundation for everything.
- *Your Significance*: When you understand your significance, you get in touch with the purpose and the greatness for which you were created.
- *Your Perspective:* When you understand perspective, you can view the problems you face as steppingstones to greatness, instead of stumbling blocks to failure. The right perspective

will enable you to walk across difficulties to your destiny, instead of allowing them to stop you in your tracks.

The way that we view a situation depends largely on our emotional and psychological state of mind. When you are facing challenges that seem to have been going on for what appears to be an eternity, your emotional and psychological state can cause your perspective of the situation to be opposed to everything that you have been declaring and believing.

Winning the internal battle and taking control of your mind, will, and emotions are key to having a healthy I-Factor

Why Have You Forsaken Me?

Matt. 27:46(b) "My God, My God, why have you forsaken Me?"
(NKJV)

I was at a low point in my life, during the writing of this book. It was one of the lowest and most difficult seasons that I had ever faced. I lost material possessions in the thousands of dollars because I had financial commitments that I was unable to fulfill. And I, to some degree, lost credibility with some people. The pressures can be overwhelming and toxic to your faith and emotional, psychological, and relational health. This is when the battle involving the mind, will, and emotions get real. You find yourself in your garden of Gethsemane *(Matt. 26:36)*, sitting under your Juniper tree *(1Kings 19:4)*, hiding in your cave *(1Kings 19:9)*, or facing your Goliath *(1Sam. 17:45)*. What's your I-Factor? What value do you place on yourself, and how do you view your life at this point and time? Do you want to live or die? My mind wanted to tell me that I had been abandoned and forsaken by God. But, in my heart, I knew that He would never leave or forsake me.

What is my I-Factor? How do I view myself at this point, and time in my life? What is my sensory perception of myself? Do I see myself as a failure with a defeatist mentality? When you evaluate the quality of your relationship with yourself; on a scale of zero to ten with ten being the highest, where do you rank it?

When I speak of a healthy I-Factor, I'm speaking of one that's not addicted to self. An addiction to self will cause us to have a distorted view of reality because we refuse to accept the fact that we are self-medicating ego junkies.

Are you emotionally, and mentally healthy enough to ask yourself the questions in the previous paragraph and answer them honestly? Be honest, because there are times when you will have an unhealthy-healthy relationship with yourself. You will convince yourself that you are good and like who you are. But in reality, you are not healthy because you have a distorted view of who you are, and don't know what a healthy you looks like because you've been unhealthy for so long that it has become your normal.

Review the following questions and evaluate yourself on a scale of zero to ten, with ten being the highest. It may be difficult if you aren't willing to be honest and are unwilling to acknowledge the need for inner healing.

Do you see yourself as a failure with a defeatist mentality?
0 1 2 3 4 5 6 7 8 9 10

When you evaluate the quality of your relationship with yourself, where do you rank it?
0 1 2 3 4 5 6 7 8 9 10

Has your addiction to self-caused you to have a distorted view of your reality?
0 1 2 3 4 5 6 7 8 9 10

Inner Healing Impacts Your Mind, Will, and Emotions.

Your emotions and feelings do not control you; you control your emotions by transforming your thinking. Your thinking controls your emotions because emotions come from thoughts. You are not your thoughts. Taking authority over your emotions is a temporary fix that has no long term effects. One of the keys to inner healing is ending the relationships that you have with the damaged you. What are you holding on to that's an excuse to feel sorry for yourself? Working on your inner healing is something that you have to do intentionally daily.

Dr. Carolyn Driver has taught and practiced inner healing for more than thirty-eight years. Several years ago, I had the opportunity to attend a leadership workshop that she conducted for a friend of mine. I was introduced to inner healing during the workshop, and have worked closely with her in recent years. During one of our meetings with a group of church leaders, she talked about "breaking the power of shame." Your internal transformation and inner healing cannot happen if you are unwilling to acknowledge what happened and take the necessary actions to eliminate its control over your life.

REFLECTION: Are you damaged emotionally? If your answer is yes, describe what occurred that damaged you emotionally. If your answer is no, briefly explain your formula for emotional health.

REFLECTION: Describe the negative impact that emotional damage can have on a person's I-Factor.

Eph. 3:20 Now unto him that is able to do exceeding abundantly *above all that we ask or think, according to the power that worketh in us.*

Hebrews 10:35 *Cast not away therefore your confidence, which hath great recompense of reward. 36 For ye have need of patience, that, after ye have done the will of God, ye might receive the promise.*

Confession

Because I am created in the image and likeness of God, I know Whose I am, and who I am. I am fearfully and wonderfully made. I am!

Behavior Modification

Behavior Modification is the enemy of Internal Spiritual Transformation. The church, for the most part, has mastered external behavior modification but has failed to empower and foster internal spiritual transformation because its focus has been on outward behavior modification. Jesus never attempted to modify anyone's behavior, He empowered and caused the transformation to take place by promoting the spiritual agenda of God and His Kingdom, by the power of the Holy Spirit.

Behavior modification is a temporary external experience that lasts for a short period. That's why we see so many who say they believe in God and have surrendered their life to Him going through repeated cycles of spiritual frustration? It's because the spirit of their mind has not been renewed. Therefore, they haven't surrendered their will to God, and have not experienced an internal spiritual transformation. They have the same habits, are living the same lifestyles, and continue to do the same things that they've always done.

In *Acts 13:9–24*, there is a classic example of behavior modification which excluded the true transformation of the heart, and the internal restructuring of the spiritual DNA.

It is said that Simon, the formal sorcerer, believed, was baptized, and continued with Philip. When the apostles sent Peter and John to lay hands and pray for the church in Samaria to receive the Holy Spirit, Simon saw it and offered money to the apostles if they would give him the power to impart the Holy Spirit. Peter addressed him by saying, *"that he and his money would perish, and that his heart was not right in the sight of God." (Acts 8:20)*

Did Simon have a recreated spirit? If so, is it possible to have a recreated spirit (regenerated), without having a transformed heart?

REFLECTION: What, in your opinion, were Simon's enemies to transformation?

According to Webster's Dictionary, *the word transform means "to change in the composition of structure, character, or condition,"* to cause to undergo a genetic transformation; Genetic restructuring of a cell by the uptake and incorporation of exogenous DNA; to change into another substance; transmute. Pertaining to, or **influenced by geneses or origins**.

To transform is to alter the structure from an internal perspective. It's the process of ceasing to be what you have been modified to be and becoming who you were initially created to be.

Transformation is:

1. Personal
2. The willingness and ability to live beyond the limits of the fallen nature.
3. A fundamental new state of being.
4. The restructuring of your worldview.

Jeremiah 1:4 Then the word of the LORD came unto me, saying, 5 Before I formed thee in the belly I knew thee; and before thou camest forth out of the womb I sanctified thee, and I ordained thee a prophet unto the nations. 6 Then said I, Ah, Lord GOD! behold, I cannot speak: for I am a child. 7 But the LORD said unto me, Say not, I am a child: for thou shalt go to all that I shall send thee, and whatsoever I command thee thou shalt speak.

One of the greatest enemies to transformation and the purpose of God is the inability to see through the eyes of faith. Because so many are captivated and insulated by their circumstances, their circumstances become the lens that control the way they view life. The power of transformation allows a person to see beyond the physical and causes the unknown to be known as we become aware of God's original intent for our lives.

Genesis 1:26 Then God said, "Let us make humankind in our image, in the likeness of ourselves; and let them rule over the fish in the sea, the birds in the air, the animals, and over all the earth, and over every crawling creature that crawls on the earth." 27 So God created humankind in his own image; in the image of God he created him: male and female he created them. 28 God blessed them: God said to them, "Be fruitful, multiply, fill the earth and subdue it. Rule over the fish in the sea, the birds in the air and every living creature that crawls on the earth." (CJB)

There is a difference between internal transformation and external change or behavior modification. External change or behavior modification is a tool of convenience that's used for personal gain. Internal transformation is the pathway to eternal existence.

The power of transformation is the internal restructuring of your spiritual DNA!

REFLECTION: Give an example of when you let your thoughts and emotions control you. Why were your actions governed by your thoughts and emotions? Being honest with yourself is the first step to gaining victory over your emotions.

On a scale of zero to ten what's the quality of your I-Factor?

0 1 2 3 4 5 6 7 8 9 10

REFLECTION: Take an honest look into who you are, and describe the quality of your I-Factor, your internal relationship with yourself?

Life Indicators

Divide your life into chapters. (You can use blocks of years, 1-5, 6-10, and so on.) Identify the negative and positive events that occurred during each chapter and briefly describe how they have shaped your life and influenced your I-Factor (who you are).

Chapter 1 Title:

Years:

Significant Events:

Chapter 2 Title:

Years:

Significant Events:

. . .

Chapter 3 Title:

Years:

Significant Events

Chapter 4 Title:

Years:

Significant Events

Chapter 5 Title:

Years:

Significant Events:

As you reflect on the events that have shaped your life, what were the major barriers to your transformation? What principles can you apply from this chapter that have equipped you to overcome those major barriers?

TRANSFORMATIONAL POINTS

1. Unrealistic expectations can be a death sentence to the fulfillment of your purpose and destiny.
2. The ability to adequately, successfully, and humbly eliminate unhealthy relationships with people, places, and things may be challenging to start with, but it is necessary; and must be done promptly.
3. Because of our internal damages and our refusal to be honest with ourselves by acknowledging and addressing our toxic behaviors, we camouflage our greatest enemies in an attempt to be who we are expected to be because we are afraid to let the world see who we are.
4. The first step to overcoming internal barriers is to transform your perception of who you are. It's unfortunate, but many times, our perception of who we are is based on the way others see us, and who they perceive us to be.
5. "Your I-Factor is a combination of the dynamics that converge to form the totality of your relationship with you."
6. Your emotions and feelings do not control you. You control your emotions by transforming your thinking.
7. Your internal transformation and inner healing cannot

happen if you are unwilling to acknowledge what happened and take the necessary actions to eliminate its control over your life.

8. Behavior modification is the enemy of Internal Spiritual Transformation.

9. One of the unfortunate realities of the I-Factor is that unhealthy people think they are healthy, like who they are, and have convinced themselves that they are all right.

4

TRANSITIONING FOR TRANSFORMATION

C aterpillars have a chemical called juvenile hormone in their bodies that's made by their brain. Whenever a caterpillar sheds its skin and the juvenile hormone level is high, it goes to the next caterpillar stage. When the juvenile hormone level is low, the caterpillar wanders (transitions) to find a site to make a chrysalis (cocoon). It encloses or isolates itself in the cocoon and transforms into a pupa. It doesn't enter another caterpillar stage. The most interesting part is that the caterpillar has to recognize its transformational triggers and be willing to put forth the effort to transition to the place of transformation. The internal restructuring of your spiritual DNA will not take place if you are not willing to transition and position yourself for transformation.

There is no sin punished more implacably by nature than the sin of resistance to (transform) change.
- Anne Morrow Lindbergh

The process of transitioning for transformation involves letting go of the way things used to be and taking hold of the way they will subsequently become. The unwillingness, however, to release the past has proven to be a major challenge for many. In between the letting go of the old and taking hold of the new, there is a chaotic but potentially creative "neutral zone" where you are not who you used to be, but you have not matured (transformed) into who you desire to be. The three phases of the transitional process are ending, neutral, and beginning. We will discuss them in more detail a little later.

Transitions and transformations can be lonely, painful, and messy, and they can occur in isolation over time. Your ability to promptly adapt to the challenges associated with transformational transitions is critical as you strive to successfully navigate the spiritual, emotional, psychological, and physical phases of the transformational process. When you are transitioning for transformation, you'll have several opportunities to analyze where you are in the transitional process of your transformation and make the necessary adjustments.

Refusing to submit to the transitional process of transformation does not guarantee that things will stay the same. It does, however, increase the possibility of you getting stuck, and becoming stagnant because you refuse to move forward in the process. Transitional stagnation guarantees a slow death. Many of us are reluctant and are opposed to transition because it's difficult, and we don't want to let go of the part of ourselves that we are comfortable with. Our comfort zones give false signals. Refusing to move out of our comfort zones is like sitting at a railroad crossing with the lights flashing. You can see for miles in all directions that there is no train approaching, everyone around you notices that the signal is false and moves forward. You, however, are stuck in the comfort zone of uncertainty and refuse to move forward. If we lose focus and expect the new season to be like the old season because we are comfortable with the way things are, we may miss the transformational opportunity and get stuck in transition. The caterpillar that's stuck in transition dies in the cocoon and never becomes a butterfly.

Understanding the Way of Transition

Transitioning during the process of transformation is like being on a roller coaster of hope and disappointment. It would be unrealistic to paint a picture for others that presents a smooth, and uneventful transition into transformation. The truth of the matter is that transitions are painful because they involve separating from something that you are attached to. The way of transition cannot be fully understood by someone with no in-depth experience of being in transition, and successfully surviving the disenchantments that are part of the experience.

When it's far-reaching, the transitional process can make you feel like you've lost more than a piece of reality; it can make you feel like everything that seemed to be reality was simply an enchantment. That's the way I felt during a season of my life when my normal was taken away, and I found myself in a disoriented state. The transition did not simply disenchant, it took a part of my identity away. When you lose a part of your identity, you feel disoriented and lost to some degree. On the other hand, if your significance and identity are determined by a position or title, you have no identity. Your identity is who you are. Your title is what you do.

When we look at the disorientation that comes with transitioning from a different perspective, it lets us see the positives that are associated with transitioning for transformation. There are times when transitional disorientation can be the prelude to something new and exciting. I want you to stop right here and paint on the canvas of your mind a picture of what your ideal life looks like. Now see yourself living it. What did you have to transition from to transition to your desired state? Were there any emotional or physiological challenges? Disassociating and identifying with the negative events from your past can make your transition for transformation a more enjoyable experience.

DR. LARRY D CARNES

The processes of transition and transformation occur simultaneously as you separate from the old and connect to the new. This can be confusing because you will be experiencing the dual citizenship of being in between your past and your now. The key is to avoid getting stuck in your past by focusing forward. Your moment of breakthrough will take place internally before it is visible externally.

If your significance and identity are determined by a position or title, you have no identity.

Responsive and Developmental Transition

Responsive transition represents what we do to get through the situation when a specific, external change triggers something. The change occurs; Then, we respond and transition.

Developmental transition isn't triggered by external behavior modification; It's the result of an inner unfolding of who we are internally. Developmental transition starts when we recognize that there are alternatives to the status quo.

Three phases characterize each of these transitions:

- *Ending:* In the ending, we lose or let go of our old outlook, old reality, old attitude, old unproductive values, and our old self-image. You may resist the ending for a while and try to talk yourself out of what you are feeling. When we surrender to this part of the process, there may be feelings of sadness and anger.
- *Neutral Zone:* Living between the old and the new, but not being either is critical because you face the danger of getting stuck in-between. You're not who you used to be, but you aren't who you are transitioning to become. This confusing phase is when our lives feel as though they have fallen apart and gone dead. We're receiving signals from the old and the new that are unclear. Nothing feels solid in the neutral zone;

56

everything's up for grabs. It's a time when you feel like anything is possible. It can be a very creative time.

- *Beginning:* Finally, we take hold of and identify with a new outlook and new reality, as well as a new attitude and self-image. We feel like we are starting a new chapter in our lives. It may have seemed impossible to imagine a future earlier, but now life feels like it's on track again. You have a new sense of who you are, a new outlook, and a new sense of purpose and possibility.

There is a time for departure, even when there's no certain place to go.
-Tennessee Williams

As a Certified Master Transformational Leadership-Life Coach, and Coach Trainer, my niche is personal development. I am always empowering my coaching clients and life coach trainees by being "Present to the Moment" when coaching or training and encouraging the trainees to be "Present to the Moment" when engaging clients. Being present in the moment is being intimately involved in their transformational process. Developmental transitions are intentional and require that you are present in the moment. Being present in the moment is to be actively engaged in the transitional process.

In its most basic function, transition helps you come to terms with the transformational process and reorients you so that you can deal successfully with your new situations. It involves relinquishing old habits and expectations while developing new ones. By answering the following questions, you will create a map that will assist you in your transformational journey.

1. Are you transitioning for transformation, or changing (modifying behavior) for convenience?
2. Who are you transitioning from, and transforming into?
3. Why do you feel the need to transform?

The transitioning process is positioning for the termination of the old culture and the beginning of the new. Somewhere between ending and beginning is the emptiness of the neutral, the place of death and life, death to the old, and life to the new. The process of transformational development is the consolidating course that we follow as we discover who we are within the time allotted for the successful completion of the metamorphosis process.

Transitioning represents the rites of passage into transformation, the point of convergence where the altering of your core, the true essence of who you are undergoes a cellular reconstruction. When transitioning for transformation, the old isn't repaired; it's done away with, and all things become new.

> *2 Cor. 5:17 Therefore if anyone is in Christ [that is, grafted in, joined to Him by faith in Him as Savior], he is a new creature [reborn and renewed by the Holy Spirit]; the old things [the previous moral and spiritual condition] have passed away. Behold, new things have come [because spiritual awakening brings a new life].*
> *(AMP)*

TRANSFORMATIONAL POINTS

1. The process of transitioning for transformation involves letting go of the way things used to be to take hold of the way they subsequently will become.
2. Your ability to adapt to the challenges associated with transformational transitions promptly is critical as you strive to successfully navigate the emotional, psychological, and physical phases of the transformational process.
3. Refusing to submit to the transitional process of transformation does not guarantee that things will stay the same.
4. Transitions are painful because they involve separating from something that you are attached to.
5. If your significance and identity are determined by a position or title, you have no identity.
6. Dissociating from and identifying with negative events from your past will make your transition for transformation a more enjoyable experience.
7. Somewhere between ending and beginning is the emptiness of the neutral, the place of death and life, death to the old, and life to the new.

8. Transitioning represents the rites of passage into transformation, the point of convergence where the altering of your core, the true essence of who you are undergoes a cellular reconstruction.

5

THE PROCESS OF TRANSFORMATION

The process of transformation involves a series of continuous internal actions that are directed at a specific end which requires total commitment. It's the internal restructuring of the spiritual DNA. The process itself can be intimidating and painful because it forces you to revisit, and face what may have been unpleasant and challenging times in your life. Inner transformation for renewed empowerment will not happen if you refuse to accept, surrender, and commit to the process of transformation.

On a scale of zero to ten, with ten being the highest; how willing are you to commit to the process of transformation?

0 1 2 3 4 5 6 7 8 9 10

REFLECTION: Describe what you determine to be the most intimidating factor of the transformation process.

Jesus didn't have issues with His truth; He knew who He was, and understood His assignment and reason for being. Peter, James, and John had the pleasure of seeing Jesus from a vantage point that no living person had experienced before. They witnessed Jesus's transformation which allowed them to see Him in a dimension that they did not fully understand and did not realize what they were witnessing. Jesus's knowledge of who He was, His acceptance of who He was, and His understanding of who He was drove and empowered Him, not the opinion of others and who they perceived Him to be.

The seventeenth chapter of Matthew reveals what was mentioned but concealed in the sixteenth chapter. The Transfiguration of Jesus was for the benefit of His disciples. It allowed them to see who He was; God in the flesh! The process that leads to the physical revealing of who you are takes place internally through spiritual maturity and through the transformational development of your character and integrity. The procedure focuses on internal development that has nothing to do with the external presentation. The beauty of who you were created to be will not be realized if you refuse to submit to and complete the process of becoming who God created you to be.

> **Matt. 16:15** *He saith unto them, But whom say ye that I am? 16 And Simon Peter answered and said, Thou art the Christ, the Son of the living God.*

> **Matt. 17:1** *After six days Jesus took Peter, James, and his brother John and led them up on a high mountain by themselves. 2 He was transformed[a] in front of them, and His face shone like the sun. Even His clothes became as white as the light. (HCSB)*

The severing of your relationship with who you've been modified to be and the introduction to who you were created to be is determined by how willing you are, to be honest and face the truth about your reality. Receiving truth starts your journey to wholeness and to the introduction to the transformed you. There are necessary endings that must take place if you are going to successfully navigate the transformational process; because you have to end your relationship with all self-defeating thoughts. Once you commit to severing ties with the inferiority complex of the fallen and identify with the risen you, you will be introduced to the awakened consciousness of your true self.

> **1 Cor. 15:52** *In a moment, in the twinkling of an eye, at the last trump: for the trumpet shall sound, and the dead shall be raised incorruptible, and we shall be changed.*

> **Phil. 3:7** *But what things were gain to me, those I counted loss for Christ.*

> **Gal. 2:20** *I am crucified with Christ: nevertheless I live; yet not I, but Christ liveth in me: and the life which I now live in the flesh I live by the faith of the Son of God, who loved me, and gave himself for me.*

Your threshold for pain will be evaluated while navigating your transformational process. When charting the course of your transformational process, start with the assumption that your efforts to transform will create problems. We have to expect and anticipate problems and the pain that comes with transformational promotion. We may try to resist the pain, but it's necessary because pain is the fertilizer for transformation and growth. It's the process of transformation that's painful, as is the process of death. Death isn't painful; it's the process of dying (transforming), from the old and being awakened to the new, that's painful.

Pain is the fertilizer for transformation and growth.

Purification Before Transformation

God has a transformational purification process that precedes promotion. He presents opportunities that will evaluate our character and integrity as we are transitioning and becoming who we were created to be. These opportunities are designed to purify our hearts, deepen our dependence on Him, and impart spiritual and natural wisdom.

> *Matthew 16:24 Then Jesus said to His disciples, "If anyone wishes to follow Me [as My disciple], he must deny himself [set aside selfish interests], and take up his cross [expressing a willingness to endure whatever may come] and follow Me[believing in Me, conforming to My example in living and, if need be, suffering or perhaps dying because of faith in Me]. 25 For whoever wishes to save his life [in this world] will [eventually] lose it [through death], but whoever loses his life [in this world] for My sake will find it [that is, life with Me for all eternity].* (**AMP**)

The pain that's connected to the process of transformation is inevitable and unavoidable, but it isn't eternal. All people experience pain and disappointment no matter how committed they are to God, no matter how flawless their characters are. Life is full of pain. When we learn to bounce back in God's grace, our joy and equilibrium will be better. The pain of separation may at times be intense; we cannot let the pressure and pain that's connected to the process force us to abandon the values and ethics that we hold dear when facing and dealing with stressful situations. You may be going through that season of refinement right now because your passion is to transform the culture of the world, but you're facing massive difficulties. The work that you'll do requires your willingness to allow God to shape, mold, and refine you beforehand. That's a part of your preparation for internal spiritual transformation. Be empowered as you are being transformed.

Are you resisting the process of transformation because you're trying to avoid transformational pain?

The internal process of transformation that takes place does not happen instantly. It happens in phases. The word *changed* in *1Cor. 15:52* is translated as *"to change one thing for another, transformed.* The phases below show the progressions that takes place during the transformational process. The time required to complete each phase will vary based upon the individual.

Red Phase

- Stage 1: *Loss of Security:* The beginning is always the scariest because of the unknowns and the challenge to leave what's been your regular way of doing things. Your feelings are fearful, very cautious, and your behavior is crippling.
- Stage 2: *Self-Doubt:* Your lack of confidence in who you are and your ability to be more will cause you to have feelings of resistance that are accompanied by unbelievable thoughts and, an antagonizing behavior.

Yellow Phase

- Stage 3: *Loss of Comfort:* How many times have you found yourself saying, "I'm not comfortable with it?" In phase three, the discomfort of transformation becomes clear and starts to set in. This is the point where you will begin to have feelings that anticipate what's ahead; your thoughts will be scattered, and your behavior is challenging.

Pivotal Zone: When you enter the pivotal zone you are required to make one of the most important decisions of your life; it could be called "your crisis at the crossroads" because it's where you decide to return to the prison and limitations of the past or to escape by moving forward and stepping into your purpose. What you choose to do at this point sets the foundation for the next chapter of your life.

- Stage 4: *Finding:* This is the place of discovery. It's the energizing stage where you find your new identity as your expectations increase and your thoughts are measurable, and your behavior is energized.

Green Phase

- Stage 5: *Fulfilling:* This part of the phase is the courage phase where your thoughts become positive thoughts because you are transforming and are confident that you can accomplish what you set out to do.
- Stage 6: *Call to Action:* The call to action is the final stage. You have succeeded and regained your ability to think clearly. Because your thoughts are focused and your behavior is exuberating, you have a different outlook and new insights into the processes of transformation and can appreciate the past, present, and future.

Your transformed character is God's counter to the systems of the world. The process of transformation contains what I call; "The Eight P's of the Promise." They address the systematic steps of the process that lead to you walking in the fulfillment of the promises of God for your life. The Eight P's of the Promise are reflected as follows:

1. Promise
2. Process
3. Pressure
4. Pain
5. Passion
6. Purpose

7. Power

8. Privilege.

REFLECTION: Identify where you are in the progression of your transformational process and describe the challenges that have impacted you the most.

TRANSFORMATIONAL POINTS

1. The process of transformation involves a systematic series of continuous internal actions that are directed to a specific end which requires total commitment.
2. Your knowledge of who you are, your acceptance of who you are, and your understanding of who you are should drive and motivate you, not the opinion of others and who they perceive you to be.
3. The process that leads to the physical revealing of who you are takes place on the inside through spiritual and transformational maturity and the development of your character and integrity
4. The beauty of who you were created to be will not be realized if you refuse to submit to and complete the process of becoming who God created you to be.
5. The severing of your relationship with who you've been modified to be and the introduction to who you were created to be is determined by how willing you are to be honest, and face the truth about your reality.
6. Once you commit to severing ties with the inferiority complex of the fallen and identify with the risen you, you will

be introduced to the awakened consciousness of your true self.

7. Your threshold for pain will be evaluated while navigating your transformational process.

8. God has a transformational purification process that precedes promotion.

9. Your transformed character is God's counter to the systems of the world.

10. Pain is the fertilizer for transformation and growth.

6

RENEWING THE SPIRIT OF THE MIND

I thought I was losing my mind until God showed me that the mind that
I had was not the mind that He created me with, or wanted me to have.
- Dr. Larry Carnes

Y ou can be healed physically without being healed and delivered spiritually, psychologically, mentally, emotionally, or relationally by the power of the Holy Spirit. The renewing of the spirit of the mind is a spiritual renewing that has nothing to do with our intellect. It would be safe to say that our senses limit us because our senses process neuropsychologically-based upon the stimuli (our sensory perception) that we receive from the environments that we are socialized and modified in.

Ephesians 4:20 But you did not learn Christ in this way! 21 If in fact
you have [really] heard Him and have been taught by Him, just as
truth is in Jesus [revealed in His life and personified in Him], 22
that, regarding your previous way of life, you put off your old self
[completely discard your former nature], which is being corrupted

through deceitful desires, 23 and be continually renewed in the
spirit of your mind [having a fresh, untarnished mental and
spiritual attitude], (AMP)

The enemies of transformation are spiritual, psychological, and physical; the attacks, however, are launched primarily against the spirit of the mind in an attempt to keep us from becoming knowledgeable about who we were created to be. Spiritual Intelligence is the knowledge that makes us aware of who we are. The enemies of transformation do not want you to be aware of, or have an understanding of who you are in God. Embracing your authentic self and understanding of how God has empowered you are the first steps toward transformation and living in divine authority.

The foundation of transformation is the renewing of the spirit of your mind, not the alteration of your external presentation. Your transformational experience comes in the form of a thought that must be entertained and acted upon before transformation becomes your reality. What is the thought you may ask? The thought of "I am!" I am who God says I am because God says I am.

Renewing the spirit of the mind can be a challenge because it challenges us to implement God's spiritual counterculture to the worldly culture that we live in. We are instructed to transform not conform.

Transformation starts with the renewing of the spirit of the mind because the mind is the foundation of transformation. The renewing of the spirit of your mind separates you from the modified you and introduces you to the created you.

The Dual Nature of the Mind

A clear concept of the dual nature of the mind includes both a conscious and subconscious part. The conscious part is what a person knows. The subconscious part is what a person is. The conscious and subconscious are connected, but the subconscious is greater than the conscious. The connection between the conscious and subconscious can be likened to the connection between a mother and an unborn child. The child is automatically fed through an umbilical feeding cord that comes from the navel and connects the fetus with the placenta. The child has no choice in what it eats but has to eat whatever the mother eats. In the same manner, the conscious feeds the subconscious; the subconscious receives and gives birth to what it's fed.

The Conscious Mind

Your conscious mind (soul) is what you know. It reasons logically from observation, experience, and education. It, therefore, finds it difficult to believe what the five senses and inductive reason deny. The conscious is stimulated by observation and the physical sensation that's interpreted in the light of our experiences.

The Subconscious Mind

The subconscious mind reasons deductively and is never concerned with right or wrong, true or false. The subconscious receives what it's fed by the conscious and gives birth to it. We are the product of what we've fed our minds and what our spirits has given birth to. The subconscious mind can't impregnate; it will always be impregnated and give birth to what it's been fed.

The Created Mind and the Formed Brain

Understanding the differences between the mind and the brain can prove to be a major discovery in our lives. For starters, let me introduce you to a concept that God made very clear to me during a series of meetings that I was conducting in Brazil in September and October of 2019. The general theme of the meetings was "The Power of Transformation" with the emphasis being placed on the importance of an intimate relationship with the person of the Holy Spirit and the co-equality of women and men in the sight of God.

Created humanity is a spirit while formed humanity is a fleshly body. God is a Spirit; therefore the mind of God is Spirit, not flesh. The renewing of the spirit of the mind is the holistic approach to transformation that doesn't involve the natural brain because a spiritually renewed mind has escaped the neurological limitations of the senses that were brought about due to being spiritually separated from God. The renewing of the spirit of the mind requires both spiritual and psychological reengineering. Therefore, when the spirit of the mind is renewed, it is no longer restricted by fleshly failure.

While the brain cannot be renewed, neurologists say the brain does have the ability to reorganize and heal itself by forming new neural (nervous system) connections throughout life. This procedure is known as neuroplasticity. Neuroplasticity allows the neurons (nerve cells) in the brain to compensate for injury and disease and to adjust their activities in response to new situations or changes in their environment. In essence, it speaks of our sensory perception (senses) becoming the compass by which we navigate life. As we objectify the shortcomings of allowing our sensory perceptions to be the compass by which we navigate life, we discover that our sensory perceptions limit us, and can be an impairment and debilitating if it negatively impacts our faith.

The renewing of the spirit of the mind is both spiritual and psychological reengineering. Therefore, when the spirit of the mind is renewed, it is no longer restricted by fleshly failure.

The Power of Attitude

Attitudes are our established ways of responding to people and situations based on what we have learned, our beliefs, values, and assumptions. Attitudes manifest through our behavior. Your attitude is the external expression of your internal spirit and beliefs (the subconscious you).

*1 Corinthians 1:1 And I, brethren, could not speak unto you as unto spiritual, but as unto **carnal**, even as unto babes in Christ. 2 I have fed you with milk, and not with meat: for hitherto ye were not able to bear it, neither yet now are ye able. 3 For ye are yet carnal: for whereas there is among you envying, and strife, and divisions, are ye not carnal, and walk as men?*

The spirit of leadership is attitude. A leader's transformed spirit or attitude makes them different from the average follower. A leader with the proper attitude will always be successful in conquering challenges. They may not be the strongest, the smartest, or the biggest, but if they have the right attitude, they can conquer any challenge that they face. A successful leader with a proper attitude has a spirit that is similar to that of a lion.

An army of sheep led by a lion will always defeat an army of lions led by a sheep.
- Dr. Myles Munroe

Romans 12:2 And do not be conformed to this world [any longer with its superficial values and customs], but be [c]transformed and progressively changed [as you mature spiritually] by the renewing of your mind [focusing on godly values and ethical attitudes], so that you may prove [for yourselves] what the will of God is, that which is good and acceptable and perfect [in His plan and purpose for you]. (AMP)

Romans 12:2 Don't become like the people of this world. Instead, change the way you think. Then you will always be able to determine what God really wants—what is good, pleasing, and perfect. (God's Word)

A leader with the right attitude is powerful because that leader can transform those who are timid into spiritually healthy leaders. A spiritually healthy leader with a transformed mind (soul) can walk into a room of people who appear to be depressed, and within twenty minutes, empower them to become an unbelievable powerful army. Transformed leaders do not use fear or intimidation to get things done through people. They get things done through people because they have earned the respect of the people.

> **Philippians 2:4** *Let each of you esteem and look upon and be concerned for not [merely] his own interests, but also each for the interests of others. 5 Let this same attitude and purpose and [humble] mind be in you which was in Christ Jesus: [Let Him be your example in humility:]* (AMPC)

Attitude is a product of belief. You cannot have an attitude beyond your belief; therefore, your attitude comes from your belief system. A transformed leader is an effective leader because of what the leader thinks about herself or himself.

> **2 Corinthians 4:3** *But if our gospel be hid, it is hid to them that are lost: 4 In whom the god of this world hath blinded the minds of them which believe not, lest the light of the glorious gospel of Christ, who is the image of God, should shine unto them.*

The spirit of your mind is renewed by feasting on the Word of God and declaring it over your life. That is not to say that darkness will go away without a battle. The question then becomes, how do we renew the spirit of the mind? The spirit of the mind is renewed by meditating on the Word of God, giving place to the Word of God in our lives, and allowing the Holy Spirit and the Word to foster transformation in the spirit of the mind.

The Law of Reversibility

The Law of Reversibility is based on the principle of Inverse Transformation. Inverse Transformation speaks of the reversal in position, order, direction, or tendency. The ability to call things that be as though they were not is to exercise spiritual authority. The inverse transformation is exercised when we call those things that be, as though they are not! When we internally objectify our desired results by faith and are not moved negatively by sight, we initiate the process of reversibility. The Law of Reversibility isn't an intellectual principle; it's a spiritual reality that's realized after the transformational internal restructuring of your spiritual DNA.

If a physical fact can produce a spiritual and psychological state, a spiritual state can produce a psychological and physical fact.

The Law of Reversibility is a spiritual principle that says the fallen spirit of the mind can be reversed and renewed.

TRANSFORMATIONAL POINTS

1. You can be healed physically without being healed and delivered spiritually, psychologically, emotionally, and relationally by the power of the Holy Spirit.
2. Our senses limit us because our senses process neuropsychologically based upon the stimuli (our sensory perception) that we receive from the environments that we are socialized and modified in.
3. Spiritual Intelligence is the knowledge that makes us aware of who we are, the enemies of transformation do not want you to be aware of, or have an understanding of who you are in God.
4. Your transformational experience comes in the form of a thought that must be entertained and acted upon before transformation becomes your reality.
5. Renewing the spirit of the mind can be a challenge because it challenges us to implement God's spiritual counterculture to the worldly culture that we live in.
6. The conscious is stimulated by observation and the physical sensation that's interpreted in the light of our experiences.

7. We are the product of what we've fed our minds that our spirit has given birth to.

8. The renewing of the spirit of the mind is both spiritual and psychological reengineering.

9. "An army of sheep led by a lion will always defeat an army of lions led by a sheep."

10. The spirit of the mind is renewed by meditating on the Word of God, giving place to the Word of God in our lives, and allowing the Holy Spirit and the Word to foster transformation in the spirit of the mind.

11. "If a physical fact can produce a spiritual and psychological state, a spiritual state can produce a physical and psychological fact."

7

THE BENEFITS OF TRANSFORMATION

I can personally attest to the benefits of transformation, the internal restructuring of our spiritual DNA, and the impact that it has on our lives if we are willing to submit to the spiritual, psychological, and emotional processes of transformation. The benefits of transformation are game-changers. They will not, however, be realized in our lives if we refuse to surrender to the processes of transformation.

The process of transformation can be a tedious journey. I would encourage you, however, to enjoy the journey as much as you can because there's the possibility of you quitting if you attempt to look too far ahead as you navigate the journey. Yes, reaching your destination is important; the joy, however, is in the amazing adventures that you will encounter, and the lessons learned during the journey.

The benefits of transformation are the recolonization of humanity back to God through Jesus, by the power of the Holy Spirit, the internal reconstruction of humanity's spiritual DNA, and, the personal and collective re-establishment of the Kingdom of God. It's the Optimum Return of God's Original Intent for humanity and the Earth.

Transformation Through Recolonization

Remember that "Recolonization is the act of re-establishing the king's governmental authority, influence, rule, and culture after it has been interrupted."

God created every human being with the express purpose of revealing His nature in humanity on Earth. He's very clear as to why He created them. The original plan of God was to extend His Heavenly Kingdom by establishing His Kingdom on Earth. In addition to God's plan to extend His Kingdom, He wanted to establish the authority of His Kingdom. The way that God recolonized Earth was to establish humanity as His administrative authority.

God's original intent was to bring heaven to Earth through recolonization, the initial disconnect between heaven and earth is documented in *Genesis 1:1-2.* God created humanity and empowered them to reestablish His governmental rule on Earth. When Adam and Eve decided to disobey God, they cut off the governmental authority and the provisions of heaven. The Kingdom of God, His authority, and the provisions of heaven were no longer established on the Earth. When this happened, humanity and the Earth declared its independence from God through decolonization.

> *Genesis 1:26 Then God said, "Let us make humans in our image, in our likeness. Let them rule the fish in the sea, the birds in the sky, the domestic animals all over the earth, and all the animals that crawl on the earth." 27 So God created humans in his image. In the image of God he created them. He created them male and female. 28 God blessed them and said, "Be fertile, increase in number, fill the earth, and be its master. Rule the fish in the sea, the birds in the sky, and all the animals that crawl on the earth."(GW)*

The Power Of Righteous Recolonization

Identification by creation deals with the legal side of redemption; it unveils and reveals what God did in Christ for us from the cross to the tomb and from the tomb until He sat down at the right hand of the Father. Humanity was created in the image and likeness of God. Therefore, our identification by creation is directly connected to God and who He is. Humanity' identification with God is a spiritual identification that has nothing to do with the physical man. God is spirit. There's nothing about God that's physical. If you've been attempting to connect with or identify with God from a physical perspective, you've been wasting your time because God is spirit. Therefore, your connection with God, your relationship with God, and the intimacy that you will experience with God is a spiritual intimacy that has nothing to do with you physically.

The benefit of transformation is God's spiritual romance of redemption through Jesus by the power of the Holy Spirit and the recolonization of humanity. It's the renewing of our covenant with God and the renewing of our passion with God. It's the benefit of being conscious of and understanding our true identity.

The Spiritual Recolonization of Humanity

My dear friend, the late Archbishop Veron Ashe, was an accomplished theologian and so full of revelation that it was mind-blowing to sit and talk with him in the wee hours of the morning after our meetings had concluded. I remember a conversation that we had on one occasion that gave insight into God's original intention for humanity. He said, *"Our purpose is to find our identity within the context of God's identity; because we can't know who we are until we know who He is."*

The only way to experience the *Optimum Return*, which is the spiritual recolonization of humanity back to God is through the Son of God. Without Jesus, there is no Optimum Return, no spiritual recolonization of humanity to God.

The Son of God became the Son of man so that the sons of man could become the sons of God.
-Archbishop Veron Ashe

John 3:16 "For God so [greatly] loved and dearly prized the world, that He [even] gave His [One and] [a]only begotten Son, so that whoever believes and trusts in Him [as Savior] shall not perish, but have eternal life. (AMP)

"Our purpose is to find our identity within the context of God's identity; because we can't know who we are until we know who He is."
Archbishop Veron Ashe

The Provision of Salvation

What I am about to say may send you into spiritual shock, but, the provision of salvation has more implications than just going to heaven. The provision of salvation is God's redemptive plan for the recolonization of humanity back to God. Salvation is transformational because it involves both death and life. This death comes from the inherent sinful nature through Adam; greater, however, is the grace of God and life through Jesus Christ our Lord. The provision of salvation is the recolonization of humanity back to the Father, and the manifestation of the Kingdom of God on the Earth. It's the reestablishment of the governmental rule of God on Earth.

2 Cor. 5:17 Therefore if anyone is in Christ [that is, grafted in, joined to Him by faith in Him as Savior], he is a new creature [reborn and renewed by the Holy Spirit]; the old things [the previous moral and spiritual condition] have passed away. Behold, new things have come [because spiritual awakening brings a new life]. (AMP)

The work of Jesus on Earth is called the atonement. It involves the removal or covering of man's sin by His substitutional sacrifice that provide a means by which humanity becomes one with God. God, through Jesus by the power of the Holy Spirit, recolonizes humanity, and; humanity recolonizes the Earth.

Your Personal Eschatology

Your eschatology addresses your predetermined assignment(s) in life and involves a course of events that will ultimately lead to the fulfillment of your destiny if you cooperate with God's plan. Christian eschatology is the study concerned with the ultimate end of the world and the destiny of the Body of Christ and the created order of God based primarily upon biblical texts within the Old and New Testaments. Your eschatology addresses your life assignment and what God has empowered you to do on Earth.

> *Jeremiah 29:11 For I know the thoughts that I think toward you, saith the Lord, thoughts of peace, and not of evil, to give you an expected end.*

The specificity of who you are is determined by God before the foundation of the earth. The family that you are born into, your siblings, your nationality, and your race are all predetermined by God. Having a reformation of clarity as it relates to whose' you are, and understanding your Kingdom assignment is essential if you are going to fulfill the purpose of God for your life.

The power of choice is that God does not control us; or force us to do anything. He gives us the option to obey or disobey. The decisions that we make in life will directly impact the plan of God for our lives. The rich young ruler, Samson, Judas, Gehazi, and the unnamed servant to Elijah that allowed him to go into the wilderness alone, all made decisions that may have negatively impacted their lives and disrupted their eschatology. We know that Judas was negatively impacted because he decided to betray Jesus. The Apostle Paul, on the other hand, made a decision that launched him into his divine purpose and destiny; and the fulfillment of his eschatology.

How do you uncover and discover your divine purpose in life? *The first step* to uncovering and discovering your purpose is to spend quality time with God, Jesus, and the Holy Spirit. You must have an intimate and personal encounter with the Person of the Holy Spirit. He will introduce you to Jesus, and Jesus will introduce to the Father. *The second step* is to stop disqualifying yourself. You disqualify yourself when your love for where you are; is greater than your passion for where you want to be. *The third step* is to discover your passion. Your Passion is the pathway to your Purpose.

Your life has been designed by God. You are not a mistake!

The Recolonization of Earth

Redeemed humanity functions as God's vice-regents, and have been empowered to reconcile the Earth to God. The world's system seeks to govern itself without acknowledging God and, in doing so, has fallen into a lost state due to its misconception of God and His Kingdom. The recolonization of the Earth to God is the responsibility of redeemed humanity. God fulfilled His responsibility when He gave His only Begotten Son. Jesus summarized it all when he said, *"It is finished."*

A colony is a territory that comes under the control of a ruler and its governing system. It's called an imperialistic authority. When the imperialistic authority of the ruler extends beyond its borders, it colonizes other territories. The essence of colonization is to make the territory that's being colonized just like the ruling country. To colonize is to extend the influence of the colonizer so that the thing being colonized will become just like the colonizer. God's original intent was to colonize Earth with heaven. He did not want to bring Earth to heaven. He wanted to bring heaven to Earth.

God created and empowered humanity to recolonize and reestablish His governmental rule and authority on Earth as His representatives. He has empowered and entrusted humanity with the authority to recolonize the Earth in His stead. *"The earth is the Lords and the fullness thereof"(Psalm 24)*. The Kingdom of God in you does not come with physical observation, it's the impregnation and restructuring of your spiritual DNA. It's the indwelling presence of God, Jesus, and the Holy Spirit living in you to recolonize the Earth.

> *John 17:17 Sanctify them in the truth [set them apart for Your purposes, make them holy]; Your word is truth. 18 Just as You commissioned and sent Me into the world, I also have commissioned and sent them (believers) into the world. 19 For their sake [e] I sanctify Myself [to do Your will], so that they also may be sanctified [set apart, dedicated, made holy] in [Your] truth. 20 "I do not pray for these alone [it is not for their sake only that I make this request], but also for [all] those who [will ever] believe and trust in Me through their message, 21 that they all may be one; just as You, Father, are in Me and I in You, that they also may be one in Us, so that the world may believe [without any doubt] that You sent Me. 22 I have given to them the glory and honor which You have given Me, that they may be one, just as We are one; 23 I in them and You in Me, that they may be perfected and completed into one, so that the world may know [without any doubt] that You sent Me, and [that You] have loved them, just as You have loved Me. (AMP)*

The successful recolonization of the Earth can not be accomplished without the Person of the Holy Spirit. He's the essence of the trinity and the transforming agent of God. It's Christ (The Anointed One) in you that's the hope of glory, and Christ lives in us in the Person of the Holy Spirit. Humanity can not be recolonized without the active participation of the Holy Spirit because He is the breath that God breaths to give life.

The songwriter wrote, *"This is the Air I breathe, "Your Holy Presence "living" in me, and I'm empty without You."* The Holy Spirit is the presence of God and Jesus living in us. He's the Life of God that causes' us to come alive.

Pastor Dan Rhodes wrote a series of teachings entitled *The Holy Spirit and You: He's More than You Think.* His latest book is entitled The Holy Spirit Imperative. In his teachings, he brings to light the active involvement of the Holy Spirit in our daily lives. Pastor Dan Rhodes lets us know that the Holy Spirit is not your "conscience," but He can awaken your ethical principles and remind you of who you are and God's righteous intentions for you. Pastor Rhodes brings light to the reality of the Person of the Holy Spirit.

The Earth will be recolonized when humanity is recolonized through internal spiritual transformation and becomes aware of who we are in God. The recolonization occurs when we are penetrated and impregnated by the Person of the Holy Spirit. Enjoy the journey as you are Empowered and Transformed by the internal spiritual impregnation and restructuring of your DNA.

You disqualify yourself when your love for where you are is greater than your passion for where you want to be.

"The Spirit of the Lord is upon Me because He has anointed me."

LIVE IN YOUR POWER!
THAT'S THE POWER OF TRANSFORMATION!

TRANSFORMATIONAL POINTS

1. The benefits of transformation are game-changers. They will not, however, be realized in our lives if we refuse to surrender to the processes of transformation.
2. The benefits of transformation are the recolonization of humanity back to God through Jesus by the power of the Holy Spirit.
3. Enjoy the journey as much as you can because there's the possibility of you quitting if you attempt to look too far ahead as you navigate the journey.
4. Identification by creation deals with the legal side of redemption; it unveils and reveals what God did in Christ for us from the cross to the tomb and from the tomb until He sat down at the right hand of the Father.
5. Humanity's identification with God is a spiritual identification that has nothing to do with the physical man. God is spirit, there's nothing about God that's physical.
6. "Our purpose is to find our identity within the context of God's identity; because we can't know who we are until we know who He is."
7. The provision of salvation is God's redemptive plan for the

recolonization of humanity to God. Salvation is transformational because it involves both death and life.

8. Having a reformation of clarity as it relates to whose you are, and understanding your Kingdom assignment is essential if you are going to fulfill the purpose of God for your life.

9. The successful recolonization of the Earth can not be accomplished without the Person of the Holy Spirit.

10. The Earth will be recolonized when humanity is recolonized through internal spiritual transformation, and become aware of who we are in God.

BIBLIOGRAPHY

God's Counterculture Copyright © 2017, Daniel C. Rhodes – Destiny Navigators, LLC

Identification: A Romance in Redemption (Twenty-Sixth Printing). E. W. Kenyon, Kenyon Gospel Publishing Society. 2012.

Leadership Pain: The Classroom for Growth., Samuel R. Chand. Thomas Nelson, Inc. © 2015

Resurrection by (Third Printing). Neville, DeVorss & Co. 1971.

Spiritual Intelligence, Knowing God and Making Him Known (Second Printing). Kirby and Sandra Clements, Clements Family Ministries, March 2013.

The I-Factor: How Building a Great Relationship with Yourself is the Key to a Happy, Successful Life. Vanable H. Moody, II. Thomas Nelson. 2016.

The Power of Your Subconscious Mind. Joseph Murphy. Wilder Publications. 2007.

Bibliography

The Search for Significance. Robert S. McGee, Thomas Nelson, Inc. 1998, 2003.

The Way of Transition. William Bridges. DaCapo Press. 2001.

Thy Kingdom Come: The Kingdom of God Now and Forever. Kirby Clements Sr. Clements Family Ministries. 2015.

ABOUT THE AUTHOR

The birth, educating and rearing of Bishop Larry D. Carnes took place in Chattanooga, Tennessee, where he was raised along with his two sisters by their parents. Bishop Carnes learned the value of honesty, respect for others and the power of service from his mother. His road to becoming the transformational servant leader that he is today started in Augusta, Georgia, where he received Jesus as his Lord and Savior.

Dr. Carnes has a unique and dynamic call of God on his life to teach God's Word with an anointing that causes the Word to come alive as it impacts lives. His teachings give spiritual insight into God's Word as mysteries are unfolded, and lives empowered and transformed. The anointing on Dr. Carnes has apostolic authority with a prophetic edge that empowers, transforms and speaks life into hearers and readers alike. These encounters result in the uncovering of purpose and destiny.

Bishop Carnes travels throughout the world assisting senior leaders by laying spiritual foundation, setting structure and teaching the importance of taking your rightful place as God's extension in the earth. His teachings have stirred and enlightened many. The Word taught by Bishop Carnes causes a God consciousness, "an awesome awareness of who the believer really is that cannot be denied."

He is a leadership coach and transformation strategist who's devoted to empowering and transforming the lives of others as he assists and helps them fulfill their purpose and destiny.

Dr. Carnes proclaims the Kingdom is now, the Power is now, and the Glory is now, because "as He is, so are we, in this world."

ADDITIONAL RESOURCES

Other Books Written by Dr. Larry D. Carnes

The Law of Servanthood
The Law of Humility

Coaching & Consulting

Optimum Leadership Coach Consultancy
The Academy of Transformation

Broadcasts

The Power of Transformation Broadcast
Preach The Word Worldwide Network TV
Saturday 9:30pm EST
Larry Carnes Ministries (Facebook)
Sunday 10:30pm EST